# Conversations with the Heart and Soul

By

Lacey A. Odoms

Conversations with the Heart and Soul
by Lacey A. Odoms

Lacey Odoms
P.O. Box 474
Marrero, LA 70073

Published by Volo Press Books, LLC
Cover Illustration by Chaz Ortega
Cover Design by Lacey A. Odoms
Editing and Formatting by Volo Press Books, LLC
Conversations with the Heart and Soul
Library of Congress Control Number: 2019938588
ISBN: 978-1-7337377-0-8

10 9 8 7 6 5 4 3 2 1
1. Poetry - American 2. Poetry - Women 3. Poetry –
African American

First Edition

Printed in the United States of America

*crippled love cannot speak*
*when the words are buried deep within*
*dying to utter what's been confined*
*trying eagerly to unburden the soul*
*yet, the war rages within*
*making its way to the outer parts through you and I*
*wrapped in*
*hate,*
*pain,*
*anger,*
*violent acts,*
*unforgiveness,*
*until we begin a conversation*
*with the heart and soul*
*and*
*love*
*can*
*spill forth.*

## In Dedication

*To my loved ones, family and friends who believed I could and reminded me of my own greatness.*

*To all the beautiful souls in the world.*

*Before you can live up to your full potential, you must step out on faith and obtain a vision bigger than you. The greatest revenge isn't the battles we fight but the battles we let go. For in doing so, we free ourselves of negative, wasted energy and win the battles we would've lost.*

# CONTENTS

# UNMASKING RACISM AND HATE

Racism and hate are viruses that have plagued not only the United States, but countries all over the world. Racism has crippled families, slaughtered innocent lives, and held the world hostage. The time has arrived for us to acknowledge the existence of racism and hate and do away with them so we as a people can unite as one. Let us allow our differences to make us unique rather than enemies.

*Violence on one individual in honor of another person's death does not eradicate the person's death nor does it bring about true justice. Only peaceful unity from every gender, nationality and ethnic group can bring about true justice, putting to rest hate, racism, violence and a need for justice.*

## we helped build this land

how can i grow?
when you keep stabbing me between my thighs
as you feed, my offspring lies
speaking as if i never existed
covering the fact
i helped build this land you call home

oh, beautiful america
with your captivating eyes
memorizing hips
your alluring lips speak of the price i paid
just to give birth to a nation
who refuses to acknowledge my name

## playing the race card

they say we're playing the race card
as if we were ever in the league
we wake up black
we do not select
when to turn on and off our blackness
if all lives matter
why do cops pull the trigger
before they question a person of color?
what happened to the crack bill of the 80s when
crack flooded black communities?
destroying black homes
but it was really you playing the race card
all along

this people of color and white issue has long been
a debate
before i was conceived
before my grandparents' grandparents made
mississippi
their home
before blacks had a voice
before slavery was an honest trade
at least in the eyes of unrighteous men
race relations with people of color was never intact
not in america
go ahead make america great again
with you
pursuing and confronting
never trying to communicate
cops
killing on contact

who cares if he was hispanic and only 13 years old
or she was just 10
when the police ambushed her home
stealing her life
apologizing
only to confess
they had the wrong address
we're tired of fighting on the front lines
here at home
with you pursuing us
like we're in combat
in full gear
we're fighting
but our only weapon
is the weapon of words
still in america

## justice is blind, standing your ground

my killer walks free as my blood screams out
on the vibrant green grass
"justice is blind
justice wasn't meant for my kind
justice wasn't meant for me"
my killer walks free as the world watches with
closed eyes
the media feeds on my death like it's thanksgiving
dinner leftovers
it's ironic my death is even up for debate

"standing your ground" cost me my life
you, my killer, walk free standing your ground

you watched
you waited
to kill me
now my death rests in your hands
my blood lingers in the air
as you—my killer—walk free
justice is blind

my killer walks free
justice is blind
it denied me the chance to "stand my ground"
justice is blind

it allowed my killer to "stand his ground"
in the name of covering the ground with my innocent
blood
justice wasn't made for my kind

my killer walks as freely as my blood screams out
on the vibrant green grass
"Justice is Blind."

## guilty of d.w.b. (driving while black) suspicious suspect

*(pull over boy, step out of the car and keep your hands where i can see them)*

what is my crime officer?
i just was trying to walk the line, officer
i have done nothing wrong, officer

don't shoot, officer
i am an unarmed man, officer
i am badly injured and unable to move

i can't breathe
the smell of death surrounds me
i can't breathe
i'm dying
you're killing me, please stop, stop shooting
your bullets are terrorizing my body
why am i pleading for my life?
i am guilt of nothing
that would cause me my life
stop shooting, i'm of no threat to you
officer
my skin color is not a weapon
why do you fear me?
you were supposed to protect me
protect me from racist crimes like this
so, why are you still firing, officer?
my innocent blood rest in your hands, officer
all i was trying to do is make it home from work to

my wife and unborn child,
officer!

officer, you slaughter me like cattle for a feast while
the world watch
on facebook live

## history in the making

we are making history

from sand beneath our toes
honey dripping from our lips
to slave ships
we are making history

from auction posts
to plantation fields
we are making history

from cotton fields
to slave masters' beds
we are making history

from the underground railroad
to freedom at last
we are making history

from jim crow laws
to dangling in trees
we are making history

from back seat riders
to freedom writers
we are making history

from the harlem renaissance
to black power
we are making history

from oppression
to freedom of choice
we are making history

from the supreme court
to the presidential suite
we are history in the making
we are rewriting history

one voice
one heart
one person, at a time

## life's circle

i fall
broken, scorned
soul, shatter
i rise
pieces are gathered
mended together
i fall
burdens of this world break me
faith diminishes
spirit crumbles

i rise
transforming the world to see me
not as man or woman
not as black or white
not as jew or catholic
not as muslim or christian
not as sinner or saint
but as a human, with a heartbeat like yours

i fall
overcompensating for what i lack
trying to prove you wrong

i rise
bringing martin's dream to fulfillment
i rise
elected the first black president

i rise
rising to the occasion

i am a fierce black woman
standing, own my own
upon your backs i rise
i rise
carrying the torch
passing it to the next generation

i fall, i rise
we fall, we rise
we are here
see us rise

## we are

we are
kings and queens
God-fearing
kingdom-walking
new-world-exploring
before there was a columbus
civilization establishing
revolution leading
barriers breaking
we are black
whatever we touch turns to gold
for our creative minds
lead to innovations
we are black
our shades of color are endless
from vanilla bean
to dark espresso
with a hint of dark blueberry glaze
our shades of color are God divine
we are black
our hair is our crown
whether it's tucked away
under a wig
like our egyptian ancestors
or free
untamed,
unkempt and beautiful
we are black

we have our own swag
we are the very essence of rhythm

we are black
we are black

we are bold
we are fierce
we are beautiful
we are intellects
we are black
we need no validation
we know who we are
we are greatness
we are black

**allow me to plead my case**

raped by a new orleans police officer
who swore to serve and protect me
served me up hiv
with a touch of the clap
15 stitches in the shape of a knife
outline the wall of my vagina

serve and protect

protected my mind from obtaining sanity
and my mouth from screaming out badge #1735

serve and protect

your seed invaded my womb
despised its existence

sitting on the examination table
nurse johnson with a police officer guarding the door
ushered me to explain what occurred moments
before

"one of his brothers took my body
inflicting pain, no man can bear
infecting my soul"

"he does this all the time
don't worry madam
he's seeking help," explained the officer
his words spin within my dome
seconds later, the perpetrator entered the room

a devilish smile beamed in his eyes
anger and terror rushed through my hollow-shell
eyeing his beretta 92f
i rescued it from his hip
emptying 15 bullets into his flesh
and one through my head
in an attempt to salvage my mind
yet, i survived the blow
how ironic is that?
now, i'm doing double life in st. gabriel
taking the life of the officer
who swore to
serve and protect me

## virginity for sale

"virginity for sale"--
any bids, highest bidder walks away with a girl- -
once hopeful
but, under your command of pleasure

my virginity is bargained and sold
like stocks on the new york stock exchange
buy low,
sell high
that's the name of the game
my vagina will determine his return on investment
the number of men that can enter my well
multiplied by how fast i can master this trade
sets the stage for this life a young man said
i was predestined to lead

"virginity for sale,
come one,
come all
get it while it's still fresh and tame"

her purity drips from her cheek
creating a flow of rain

"virginity for sale"--
$250, sold-- black girl with unique eyes

"15 just right, by age 25 you'll make me a
millionaire"

man after man enters her well

after the 5<sup>th</sup>, her body lies numb
blood runs down her thighs onto the marble floor
once beautiful, unique eyes
now clouded by sorrow, pain, anguish
tears of crimson slide across her disfigured face
impregnated with a seed that shall never breathe
such polluted air
he dies in his mother's womb
as she enters heaven's door, never reaching 25 years
old

"virginity for sale- -
come one,
come all. "

## imprisoned mentally

you lurk
peeping through her
soul
you teach
creating monsters
disrespectful boys
men
that give into their own lust
and greed
training them
to compensate for what they lack
through male dominance
trying to remold the giver of life
to nothing more than a
cheap thrill
toy mannequin
used for sexually penetration
sexual advances go unwanted
unnoticed
ambushed by your hand
griping her vagina
she screams out and push you away
you smile
self-gratification taking control

how could you?
it was a uterus like hers
that gave you life
i watch her face turn red
as water rushed
from her eyes,

suicidal thoughts immersed throughout her mind
broken
raped
living in a world where men and power
have no regard for women and girls
she's
we are
just toy mannequins
at your disposal

## woman i am

woman i am
i am more than
what the eyes behold
woman i am
i am more than these breasts and hips
i am more than these lips
woman i am
i am more than my feminine ways
woman i am
i am more than what lies between my thighs
woman i am
i am more than my outer core
i am so much more
woman i am
i am the ceo of a multibillion-dollar company
i am a poet, mathematician, financial analyst,
surgeon, lawyer, teacher, war hero…
woman i am
i am mother of men
mistress of love
advocate of human rights
peacekeeper of war
woman i am
i am that intermittent light that passes between
man and God
yes, i am woman

# GATEKEEPER TO LIFE'S ENCOUNTERS

Love, death, pain, religion, hate, violence and depression are words, emotions and behaviors we as humans engage in daily. Regardless of ethnicity, gender, nationality or personal status we all are unable to escape life's pleasures and sorrows. Trying to understand life and the people within it is a constant struggle of mankind.

## caught up and didn't know it

he caught me
hell, i didn't realize i was running
until i decided to give blood

"ms.," the nurse said,
"you're hiv positive."
you got to be kidding me madam
i don't sleep around
i've been with the same man since high school
i'm afraid the tests don't lie
i'll advise you to talk to your mate.

rushed home with my foot to the petal
90mph down I-10
35 minutes later, i arrived at his home awaiting
answers.

to my surprise, he had a visitor exiting his domain
questioning the individual,
his male lover, that information i later discovered.
it was revealed
they had been dating
for as long as we had been together
but, he ain't gay, i explained
"i'll be if he ain't," his lover confessed
so, you telling me he's two-timing us both
"oh, my dear you looka here
it's not uncommon for our man to dabble between
the sexes
dl brothas are a thing of the times"

and i presume aids are too
that bastard is hiv positive and i guess,
so are you!
fiery and fright filled his eyes as the words rolled off
my tongue

as the accused crossed our path,
all i could mumble was, "how could you?
i gave you 7 years of my life."

suddenly my voice became empowered with rage
"how do you repay me?
with death… that's how!
you're a walking time bomb
and i, your fiancé remained in the dark."
emotions overshadowed my judgment
3 lives were claimed that day including my own.

## just another number

see, john was my first
then there was jack
damn he had a nice 6 pack

and well, hakeem, he wore a size 10
need i say more?

but mike, he could leave a sista breathless
now, taylor invented the 12 play

a few others can along in between the various
relationships
jo, tim, carl, jack, george, john 2, 3, and 4,
will, derrick, and chris
and some others
pardon me, i can't seem to remember their names
after the 5th shot of patrón,

oh, did i mention bill

last, but not least
the only man able to claim my heart, my soul, my
body, and my mind
the father of my unborn child
he almost made me lose my mind
like a stalker in the night
i just can't shake this brotha
rain or shine he's by my side
until the end of my time

his name you ask?

his name?

he's the one
men stumble within his presence
politics play on his intellect
scientists are baffled by his existence, and the plague
he has caused
countries are destroyed with the mere mention of his
name

his name?
i thought you knew,
his name?
i believe he goes by mr. h.i.v.

## our soul lingers

our soul lingers
like the smell of milk upon a camel's tongue
we are not blood sisters
yet our hearts long to embrace cultural norms
slaughtering who we were
dying to be perfect

your once perfect God-given body now resembles a
bad replication of barbie

my destiny ticket is now your sorrow
forced fed millet with a double side of fat
stretch marks is my demon and his treasure
the plumpness of my rump and the thickness of my
thighs will be some man's pride
and i'll be his bride
before thirteen
but hush my age must go undisclosed
as my body, your body is predisposed
to a culture that defines us by how well we
can master this masquerade of lies
overflowing with hate,
self-inflicted to hide the scars that paralyzes our
spirit
hindering our ability to love self and obtain faith in
God

sister… you and i grieve
grieve for the women we will never be
grieve for the teen years that could have been but we
will never know

trying to hide the need for my mother's care
i'm torn between what's ordain to be right
and this forced fed life of skinny legs, oversized
breast, sun kissed skin and a pretty man made face

i too,
we too
are torn
torn between what's ordain to be right and this forced
fed life of thick legs,
oversized back breakin breast, sun kissed stretched
skin and a pretty plump man made face
this orchestrated smile hides the blisters we have
woven within our skin connecting our soul
as it lingers like the stench of dried blood
surrounding a bed of corpuses

## government shutdown

no appropriations
no continuing resolution
government shutdown has occurred
more like
government crackdown on the middleclass and the
poor
our government does more harm to its own then
terrorists
a government melt down has occurred haven't you
heard
it took only 435 in the house and 100 in the senate to
bring our nation to its knees
as its citizens hold their breath
wondering nervously what's next
furloughed with no pay
like my rent isn't still due
so what! the government has closed its doors on the
working class citizens
all in the name of political antics
what does it matter if my light bill is due and no
paycheck is coming through?
government crackdown on the poor
a bunch of fools sent me home with no bread to feed
my family of five
government shutdown has been declared
what a disgrace
everything has come to a halt in the land of the free
and for what to show the world who's really in
control
but yet you couldn't formulate a plan
government shutdown has occurred

haven't you heard
obamacare is the reason
wow! you would rather see the nation fail
than provide citizens with health care
government shutdown is the talk of the town
all in the name of political antics
while the terrorists lurk
and our government play tic tac toe
with our lively hood

## wasting time away equals lost lives

mothers cry as little girls wonder why
at the time of such horror,
men would force them to experience newfound
sorrow
don't they know bodies are floating throughout the
city's door?
some of those bodies belong to my family tree
in the mist of the confusion, i began to pray
trying to make sense of what seems to be an illusion
i've come to the conclusion its 2005
and, we still have yet to love our brothers
for if we did in the wake of mother nature's wrath,
there would not have been a delay
in getting the citizens of the usa
out of katrina's way
men, women, and children mainly black,
but who's looking at the color of our skin
besides george bush and his fellow men

trapped inside an attic
temperature reached over 100 degrees,
i can barely breathe
as the water covers my chin

falling asleep on rooftops
bodies drift off
making the cemeteries look like schoolyards
dead corpses filled the superdome and convention
center
new orleans was abandoned for days
maybe 12 or more

i stop counting because i knew my time was through
i've lived my life only
13 years old,
but, who really cares about the little girl they never
knew
what if this was the little girl, who lived inside of
you?

## who's to blame?

we're taking cover once again
can't believe my own eyes
swear they telling lies

9th ward and st. bernard parish levees
has been sabotaged
newspaper filled
are you for real?

my city's life is on the line
6 months at a time
and the army corps of engineers
messing around

but hey, aren't they just following
their superior's orders
government screwed us once again
with their political antics
yet it's our borders
that's keeping orders
if we go down,
this whole economy
is screwed.

## rightin' our wrong

even when i'm wrong, i'm right
but, never at the expense of you, would i wanna be
right
so, i'll be right, so i can reverse my right to wrong
and make it alright
because i must admit, our love is strong
i don't mine standing in the background
as long as you take my hand
place me on your right side
there i stand heavy laden
burden with words
thoughts of us, you, me
the throne is where i rest my crown
until the hour, our wrong will become our right
then everything will be alright


maybe when the clock chimes 12
scientist will have a cure for at least 200 cancers,
hiv will be obsolete
the sky will rain manna
food riots will be a thing of the past in haiti
the son we lost in iraq will arise from his grave
police departments will be forced to honor those they
serve
old government will surrender
their wanna be robin hood tactics
instead of stealing from the poor, while the rich get
fat
from all the lies they wrote, now they choke

in a perfect world,

society will be free from hypocrisy,
government dominance and corruption
but, since it's not i guess i'll by wrong
so you can be right
and everything will be alright
at least in my world

## zimbabwe's tarnished diamonds

"me, no blood diamonds."
maybe, if i cared too.
if you cared to,
state your name, state your claim
to this land, zimbabwe
land where precious diamonds
are transformed into blood diamonds
your diamonds
blood diamonds transformed into more diamonds
more blood
red blood
red mud
covers the corpses where weeds grow
we go
buy those diamonds
blood diamonds
zimbabwe's children crumble
in red mud, zimbabwe's mud
marange field

mai mujuru's breast
feed her vine vinegar for nutrients
gives off soot for energy
no sun, no son
no strife, no life
no diamonds
yes, diamonds
blood diamonds

zimbabwe, oh zimbabwe
the vinedresser, vine oppressor

zimbabwe, oh zimbabwe
mud vibrant red, unnatural red from
blood diamonds

black marketers and illicit miners
on the prowl for
tarnished diamonds
blood diamonds
yes, diamonds
me 5 and ¾ carat diamond.

"me, no blood diamonds."

**cataclysm**

the earthquake
shook my city port-au-prince
it shook it hard until
buildings came plummeting down
under the rubble lies my mother
she screams out to relieve her of the massive weight
a pyramid of debris 5ft high and 10ft wide is stacked
on her back
tears tumbling down my cheek onto
the debris that holds my mother hostage
for my hands are too small to carry the load off her
back
yet, i try tirelessly
she lie
i sit
we wait for death to save us
as my sister abroad awaits our faith

across the city my people are scattered
in the mist of the cataclysm
i spot a building in the distance i believe to be a safe
haven
but this is no safe haven this is a death mine
dead bodies imitating sky scrappers

staring in horror i notice
a young boy's
wrist bearing the bracelet my best friend
mother made for us
it reads "blood brothers r&l"
i look closer

a scar extends from the tip of his lip to the bottom of
his earlobe
(*it can't be him, it can't be my best friend*)
i open his eyes my spirit flees
only 9 years old
his arm hangs down
lifeless
from the 9th row of brick bodies
like a cattle at the slaughter house
too much for my stomach to tolerate
my body is still running off last month's bread
as i pour my heart over this scene,
it devours my energy
haiti
my heart bleeds for you
my soul cries out to you
my prays are with you
questioning, have we too, become a decapitate
nation?

## the anti-homosexuality bill 2009

you say you're cracking down on people like
me as if i'm a notorious drug lord
or serial killer.

condemn me if you must,
ostracize me as you please,
crucify me upon your
anti-homosexuality altar
offer up my flesh as your sacrifice
to your God of traditional family values
you have my permission to rid yourself of
my innocent blood

for i've done nothing wrong
what crime am i guilty of?
besides that which you state in your bill
i am a homosexual
who carries out my life
practicing the golden rule

if i've sinned, let
God who is in heaven
judge and acquit
me of these charges
for christ who sits on God's right hand,
is now, my lord and savior
giving me new spiritual life
pleading my case before the
true Judge
for i've done nothing wrong
to have you rob me of my earthly life

beat the blood out of me if it soothes you
maim me until my face turns blue if it will make you
whole again
bury me alive with the dead if it will console you
cram me in a toilet bowl overflowing with feces if
you think it will break me
drench my body in fresh urine if it will relieve you
force me to clean this prison on my bruised bleeding
knees if it will purge you clean
ransack my body if it will prove your masculinity
and when you are through my autopsy shall read
trauma to the rectum, congestive heart failure,
strangulation of the soul

the angel of death now lingers over you
as he watch you
uganda
gang rape a fellow activist
claiming to rehabilitate her
but all you have done uganda
is kill what remains of her
create war
heterosexuals vs. homosexuals
destroying our faith in God
all in the name of your
anti-homosexuality bill
transitioning the land of uganda from
unspoiled beauty to akeldama

**let the healing begin**

traveling through emotions of all sorts
entering into a place of hostile confusion
hate buried deep within the ribcage

forgiveness asked if i would be so bold
to join him in the pursuit of healing open wounds
out of desperation, i took him by the hand

walking into blocked off zones
atomic bombs at the end of each rope
strong enough to wipe out a whole breed of falling
priests

i begin cleaning the punctured wounds
it was like throwing salt and vinegar on eroding flesh
the pain rushed throughout my skin entering my
limbs
as tiny nerves shattered into pieces

unblocked my ribcage
opened up my heart,
my pores

watching the wounds slowly fade away
it was like trying to put humpy dumpy back together
again
not impossible with God
just time consuming for me

## a walk through three generations

when i was younger
much younger
i would wonder
who this beautiful being was
with such impeccable style
i simply knew her
as grandmother
my mother's mother
but
yet, i did not know her
it wasn't until i was older
much older
when i begin to discover her
not her simply as my grandmother or my mother's
mother
but her
besides the various roles she played
but the core of her

i discovered i was more of her than i was my mother
or maybe a blend of both
because after all my mother was her
even if she didn't realize it
my grandmother and i had a lot in common
more than i would've imagined
we would chat for hours about her life and those she
loved,
her struggles and life wonders
and how she would dance at my wedding
i recall her saying, "you have only one life baby so
live it and enjoy it"

as i shared my hopes and dreams with her and my
feelings of discouragement along the way,
she would say,
"nothing in life worth having comes easy; if it comes
easy, you don't want it"
and then we would talk some more
until sleep tried to consume me and it was time to go
in discovering her identity,
i discovered my own
and all that lies beneath the surface
like strength,
character, perseverance
integrity
love beyond measure
joy over the littlest sweetness of life
and how three generations could merge into one
her (bonnie bell), my mother (evonnie) and me
(lacey)

**why does life burden me so**

i'm tryin to do according to God's laws
turning my life around
tryin to do right
got a job, even enrolled in school
helping those in need, with little i have
no complaints here
God is good
lived to see my son's 10th birthday
lookin at him make me feel like i've done at least
one thing right

diagnosed with cancer at 33 years old
can't afford my prescription drugs
but, God carries me through
no complaints here

my car broke down
struggling to get to school
 falling behind on my lessons
yet, still managing to do good for others
no complaints here
life is beginning to press upon my heart

lord!
i'm doin all that i can
why must i endure hardships one after the other
don't you love me
i am your child
flesh of your flesh
soul of your soul
heart of your heart

take away my inflictions
don't you hear me talking?
why do i go unheard?
what is the lesson here?
i don't understand your plans

child quiet your spirit and sit awhile
lean on me, i am your crutch
believe in me, i shall give you relief
lay your burdens at my feet
i will bear the load
take my hand, i will be your guide
your pain isn't in vain
how can you say i do not love you?
i birth you into existence
flesh of my flesh
soul of my soul
heart of my heart
my spirit dwells in you
you shall make it through this season
enjoying the fruits of next harvest

## life jacket

for moments at a time, depression consumes my soul
it takes me under, without my consent or knowledge
i'm left in the driver seat with no breaks
i plead to God, but it seems he turned his ears from
me
so, i vow to turn from God, but my heart is still with
him
feeling lost and confused i shout at God
"what's the purpose of this sadness i feel; how did i
get here?
i was serving you sunday
and by monday afternoon this spirit has fallen upon
me
crippling me. is this your idea of a joke?

with my eyes flooding with tears, i whisper;
don't you hear me talking God?
why can't i hear your voice?
why are you stuck on mute? don't you love me?
i feel like i'm going insane
what's the purpose of life if i'm at war within?
i don't understand
how i can be a christian and still become depressed
without a moment's notice?

3 days later God spoke
tears filled my eyes as he spoke to me
he reminded me of his sovereignty
how it's been him carrying me all this time
then he showed me jeremiah 29:11

"for i know the thoughts that i think toward you, says the lord, thoughts of peace and not of evil, to give you a future and a hope"
i fell into him allowing him to be my life jacket suddenly depression fled and i was no longer on the edge

## dreams diminish

can dreams fade away within a flash of light?
or do we simply abandon them?

for if dreams diminish, where do they go?
moving in the wind with dancing leaves
or back to its birth place?
where we were once impregnated with visions
having a miscarriage the day before we were to
conceive

perhaps our dreams became abandoned
when we realized
dreams are the blood that keeps our hearts pumping
the reason why tomorrow is a desire

where would we be if our dreams didn't fade away?
no closer to achieving our dreams than we are today

lives traveling two roads
time still forsaking us
love entrapping us
people enhancing us
and God still carrying us

dreams aren't lost just forgotten
i thought i should be the one to remind you
to dream once more

# FROM COAST TO COAST

It does not matter where you live or your social status because we all have problems. Adversity is known from coast to coast. Some say "when it rains it pours," but they forget without rain nothing can grow and maturity is at a stand- still.

Whatever we are going through is only for a season, at the end of the season we will reap a harvest. Life was not meant to break us, but to make us stronger. It takes a courageous person to stand still in the face of adversity and an even stronger-willed person at heart to continue to walk and believe in Jesus Christ regardless of their current situation. Your pain is not in vain. A time will come when you will say, "I had to endure those heartaches, so I can be where I am today."

## sunday morning news

the sun breaks
i get ready for church
thank my heavenly father for his continuous mercies
and grace
then onto sunday morning news

i got sunday morning news on my mind
"who dat say dey goin beat those saints," says the
sports newscaster
the saints 13-0 win was quickly shattered when the
message
 "breaking news" appeared across—my—tv screen
the news reporter demeanor suddenly changed
dismayed, she blurted out
13 murders all within 12 hours
the latest occurred just moments before 8:35am
a 5 month old baby boy,
a 7 year old girl, and their
39 year old mother and father
were brutally murdered on the 400 block
of north claiborne
the 7 year old twin is in critical condition
i got sunday morning prayer on my mind

i got sunday morning news on my mind
in haiti children die from lack of food
here they die from manufactured bullets engraved
with their name
bullets laced with hate rain down on the youths of
new orleans
i got sunday morning sorrow on my soul

i got sunday morning news on my mind
9 bullets laced with hate
painted his face dirty red
he's not quite 22
not quite a man
buried before his time
his assassinator
not quite a man
not quite 22
but a cold blooded killer
his hands now scarred by dirty red blood
i got sunday morning tears in my heart

i got sunday morning news in my mind
i got sunday morning prayer on my tongue
i got sunday morning sorrow in my soul
i got sunday morning tears in my heart
while still making my way through the church doors

## i see you

sitting there
over there dumbfounded
death
struck him
down
while still a child
now you sit there over there
next to his
rotting body
thirty-six hours has passed since
seven bullets made their way into his
chest cavity, lower abdomen, frontal lobe
upper spine, wrist

risking what little faith remains in you
praying someone will hear your inner cry
for your eyes lack tears and your voice is on mute

you look down stroking your lifeless brother head
asking God why has his angles left your side

no one seems to care that mama's friend put these
death pills into her drink
no one showed up when the bullets from his toy gun
shook
the apartment my mama rented from the brown high
mice
i know they heard the loud thundering-lighting
coming from apartment 73r

this apartment is where i taught brother to count,

counting toes,
what didn't dwell in the fridge,
counting dreams, mama's spirit drinks
counting the cracks upon mama's back
we made sure not to step on mama's back
we counted the holes in the ceiling and those that
came through the back door
we counted sheep to sleep
and our numbered days
where were you lord
when our counting were taking place
where are you now that my body is drenched in air
dried blood
and my soul hangs in the balance of right and wrong
where are you lord my spirit needs
to be delivered from this place we can never call
home

## darfur cries out

please do not tell me to wait
please do not tell me to lower my voice
or quiet my inner child
please do not tell me for the thousandth time
my freedom will come soon
"freedom soon" is no longer an acceptable phase
my mother, father, brother, six sisters, newlywed
husband
died awaiting your soon
over a half a million corpses are stacked on each
other
within a grave the janjaweed arab militia built
their souls scream out in agonizing pain
chanting the names of their murders, rapists,

leader of darfur genocide
omar al-bashir
upon his neck my freedom hangs

freedom shall be mines today
not tomorrow

liberty hangs upon my tongue now
when i speak it spills forward like a tsunami
i will not quiet these waves that push ashore

my breast milk gave birth to four generations
of kings and queens
and you say, wait for freedom
we are in the middle of an ethnic cleansing
when the sudanese government is through

i'll have my freedom, so you say

unchain my feet, let go of my hands
i will declare my freedom today
slaughtering the janjaweed arab militia
and president omar al-bashir
with my words

i forgive you men of terror
i forgive you for destroying my princesses' womb
before they had time to experience their menstrual
flow
i forgive you from robbing my princes of their man
hood
on their backs
their insides were ripped apart
i forgive you for destroying my garden of eden
with your famine, diseases, blood stained sheets,
machetes carving away my soul
i forgive you for this genocide you so skillfully
devised
in an attempt to rid darfur of my african tribes

my freedom, our freedom has finally arrived
through my words which saturate this atmosphere
now

## fourth of july

fourth of july
fourth of the lie
bombs blazing into the air
over there, over here
dirty south
bombing new orleans inner city youths
scattered ashes cover the playground
the humid air carries their souls away
       drafting where no man has gone

fourth of july
fourth of the lie
bombs blazing into the air
once again
over here, over there
middle east
bombs drop
youths and mothers turn into dust
america's lustful need to cover another man's seed
families cry out- "ceasefire" yet we fire

rain unable to wash away bloodstains
gave our flag its crimson color
land of the free
ms. america was purchased for a hefty fee
your blood, my sweat, his ashes

fourth of july
fourth of the lie
sky's blue, eyes blue
spies lurking
trying their best to protect
a woman whose womb is infested with greed
polluted with deceit, plague with violence

from her flesh she birth forth a dynasty
where we gladly trade our soul
to harvest green paper back
yet, we still lack

fourth of july
fourth of the lie
how shall we rejoice when our children are
dropping like flies
before our very eyes
fourth of july
fourth of the lie

please cease fire...

## f.g.m. "female genital mutilation"

an elderly woman spoke to me
when i was three
told me a story of the passage i must undergo to
become woman.
then, she said to me,

i dream of a day when my women will be freed.
i dream of a day when my girls will be freed.
i dream of a day when my vagina will speak.
i dream of a day when my vagina will not be sewn
shut.

this is the passage you must undergo to become
woman.
something sharp to cut and remove your genitals,
as we, women hold you down while you put up a
fight.
we sew you shut but not before we remove your
pleasure spot.

this is the passage you must undergo to become
woman
preservation of your purity
mutilation of who you are
not as a person, but a woman

i dream of a day when this culture confines us not
i dream of a day when my vagina can breathe
i dream of a day when you my darling will be freed

but, for today

my vagina remains silenced to the world

within my hut at night
it screams out,
      "damn you
        let… me… breathe…"
fungus has made its home within my vagina walls
i died internally, seconds before the death angel
came to my rescue

the elderly woman spoke
this was the passage i undergone to become woman

## nuée ardente

am i not,
are you not,
are we not,

first africans, before we take on the identity of a
tribe?
yet, we are at war
fighting among brothers,
raping our daughters.

again, i ask you.
i ask myself.
are we not,
are you not,

first, an african?

then, tell the unborn why
machetes grips the palm of babies
forced to kill love ones in pursuit of false justice
girls kidnapped is becoming an ongoing
reoccurrence
to satisfy the militia sexual desires
violence has become the bread for kenya's people
men's eyes are ripped from their sockets
territory is cease within the blink of an eye
where is kenya's beauty now?
the people and their homes are like trees
consumed within the wrath of nuée ardente

**a war on my front porch**

a plague consumes the land
taking our children prisoners
standing on corners making exchanges
in between shifts, a body or two lays covered in
blood
sorrow filters the air

mothers cry out
"lord why, my babies lay victims to a lost cause"

one on his way to the morgue
while another walks through angola's doors
he didn't mean to take the life of that anonymous
boy.

words collided,
egos flared,
guns rose,
bullets pierced the flesh,
bodies fell,
sirens cleared the streets.

he was left standing over the spot where his brother
once laid
trying to fight a war that wasn't in his league.

## death row

only 15 years old,
a stab wound ended his season
his growth can no longer be completed

a mother cries as her heart crumbles
the accused teen stands in disbelief

two teen lives destroyed
one lying on the hot concrete covered in blood

the other in hand cuffs
2nd degree murder, only 16 years old
their lives just beginning

two teen lives ruined
can't even remember what started the confrontation

both teens serving a death sentence

## black youths on the verge of extinction

if violence is the problem,
what is the source?
if young black teens is the source,
what is the solution?
we need a resolution
too many, black teens are doin life on death row

are the people of new orleans blind?
do they not see a problem exist here?
how many black boys must end up in the cemetery
before we lend them a helping hand?
how many black children must go fatherless?

selling drugs is becoming mandatory
can't hold down a 9 to 5
that isn't payin minimum wage

neglecting to give them an education
the illiteracy rate is reaching an all-time high.

i know a solution
put them behind bars
statistics state they'll end up there anyway
so why not get paid
open the front gates
welcoming our prospective future generation
to the home of the dead

is this not a form of genocide?
are we blinded by our own greed
or lack of social concern?

**in response to your dis': a continuation of "black
youths on the verge of extinction"**

so, you continue to sleep
denying our black youths
leading them to a life of demise
the same the nazis did to the jews,
and the hutu tribe did to the tutsi tribe.

but what is this you say?
you are not murders
how dare i imply such a thing?

oh, but you are
slaughtering thousands
corpses filling the landmines within new orleans wall
all because you refuse to lead the teens
who are crying out in pain
for your right hand.

   now, i understand!

   obviously, you can't relate since you
   neglected to perceive
   by ear the knowledge that leaked from my
   pen on to this paper
   thoughts my mind consumed
   and was willing to release at your assistance
   yet and still, you proclaim this knowledge
   i write is too ancient to be fulfilled
   less i remind you,
   the present and the past coincide with one
   another

so, take heed to my declaration
look closely at these words
before you decide to put away this page
i do not engage in this verbalization
for pure delight,
but for your enlightenment.

*(anonymously yours)*

## the tree speaks

i, the tree, speaks
rooted deep within the motherland
the width of my hips
disclose my age
i've lived 6 lifetimes and then some

i've witness the evil within man's heart
selling off their limbs
surrendering their sons to poverty
trading their daughters to the streets
for a few straps to get them through the night
lacking any morals

tears water my roots during the dry season, which is
year round
my leaves wither away like the dreams of babes
slowly their bodies deteriorate from malnourishment

the river is red
there is no sacred place to baptize this nation

i, the tree, speaks
speaking life
into man
helping man reverse the vicious cycle
of self-hate
purifying the waters
filling their bellies with love
putting on family values as their armor
as this nation, take a dip in the jordan river

i,
the tree
speaks.
awaiting the manifestation
of the hope that has yet to be seen.

# LOVE HAS NO FORM

The greatest gift anyone can pass on is love for God, self and mankind. It is extremely difficult to love in spite of the pain and disappointments. However, in time, with God's help, our ability and willingness to forgive and let go of past hurt will be our key to serene peace and joy.

Sometimes what we think is lost is really hidden from our sight. If you look closely, you'll discover what was there all along. Nothing is un-repairable. Hearts can be broken and mended back together again. All you have to do is allow yourself time to heal, and welcome a new love into your heart, beginning with you.

**a love letter to life**

dear beloved,

lately, i've been thinking about ending our
relationship
too much to bear,
impregnated with your seed
loving you more than i need
constantly, inflicting pain,
each day becomes harder for me to remain.
dark clouds and fallen stars overshadow my world.
eyes float in rivers of tears.
knocking me on my tail,
vowing to love me another day
keeping me within your wrath
taking hold as the sun shines,
drying up my eyes,
we smile,
making sweet memories within the blue sky
birds sing, as we dance
you take on a toil,
weighing me in.
how do i begin to mend,
this shattered heart of mine?
rain washes away the burdens
taking you in strides.
oh, how i do love you, life
but sometimes you can be hard to endure
that is when i remember,
happy days are near
there's no need to fear
for God, is here.

## after the pain

what comes after you close the door?
new love and much more

all that time you spent on old love wasn't in vain
made you stronger and wiser for a greater love to
enter your door
a love so divine
God took longer than usual to make sure you had the
very best

those other loves were nothing more than a slow
dance
going through emotions because you didn't wait on
God
so, you were given the worse of the crop
love that used, abused, misused your trust, denied
your faith

and convinced you love is: pain,
cheating and lying tongues,
time never to spare,
tears of endless sorrow and words
that makes us seek shelter anywhere but home

until that day you decided to let God play cupid
in the mist of heart-aches,
God sent you an angel
to mend your heart
and show you the love that was waiting for you all
along

## letting go

refuses to let your deeds prolong my growth
letting go of past mistakes
regrets i've encountered
forgiving you was a task i've neglected to do

restoration is what i'm in need of
healing is what my heart pleads for

letting go of the sorrow
your words can't play on my inner-being
christ is who i long for

if forgiving you is the only way i can receive his
right hand,
forgiveness is what i'll bestow upon you
just thought "you" should know
i'm finally—letting go!!!

## imagine

can you imagine if love ruled the world?
there would be no more souls losing their lives in
lost warfare,
mothers' tears will cease,
prayers will increase,
love will dominate the seasons.

if love ruled the world,
sara wouldn't be impregnated with her father's
seeds.

if love ruled the world,
there would be no more killing or stealing,
rapes will become obsolete,
war will be replaced with peace,

no more souls dying from lack of meds,
no need for africa to cry,
she can feed her land and heal her man.

**life of a newborn**

clinging to my bosom,
feeding off my soul for survival,
obtaining knowledge for tomorrow's journey,

the sun breaks as dreams began to fall,
rain splashes making way for the rainbow.

like a golden star, it leads you to a place of harmony.
with a scenery so unreal,
it'll make the devil feel at ease.

worries can't intensify, only room for love to
magnify.

## a boy's love

emotions override the shore
past lover confessing his love

the one he loves
refuse to settle for just any ordinary love affair

"do you love me, and how much he asks?"

yes, i love you
the love i bear travels past the ocean floor
to the outer limits of the lithosphere
then, it stops—
unable to travel past the universe

for now my love,
our love resides within your arms
upon your chest
there it rest
until the moment i confess out-loud
your love just ain't enough

the glare in your eyes
the smile upon your face
even your gentle touch convey love
still, it lacks committed love,
suicidal love
"not that you'll take your life for me, by no means"
but, you'll die to playaism, and self-gratifying
behavior
graduating to a man
willing, able, and ready

to stand upon God's foundation of love
that love
that transcends from your soul to mine.

**dare to love**

who will dare to love
when love has beaten you blue
left you bruised and bitter
who will dare to love
when love leaves you cold and used
vacant of comfort
who will dare to love
when love ransacks the inner you
deals you a foul hand that can't be tame

i will dare to love
love in the mist of adversity
love when the ocean hues transform from a clear blue to a
darken red
love when love's deadly drug has won me under
i will dare to love, love's tender mercies i see when i look
into my newborn eyes
i will dare to love when love turns to me with that
conniving smile
i will even dare to love america
although, she denies me of my name, ripped my soul
from within me and
and damn me to go back to a place my feet never tread
upon.
but, for the sake of love
i will surrender to hurt
and walk in love

so yes, i will dare to love
when the rain drenches my flesh
and h2o escape through my pores
love after the sun melts away my skin from my bones

i am she who dares to love the imperfectness of you

**yes, just maybe**

maybe he'll uncover me
with his hand interlocked
within mine
hanging on to my every word like it's his
life line
life support
maybe he'll see all of me
after the walls has fallen
maybe he'll be so bold
to love all of me
me, the parts of me that's kept hidden
maybe one day he'll undress me
undress me with my fathers last name
and draped me with his
maybe we'll exchange vows before our father and
savior
maybe i'll have that fairytale love
love that's so potent it takes our breath away
and it stays
pure, free, unified and unfiltered

## uncovering me

can my outer beauty still be seen
without this masquerade of lies?

strip me of this human hair
remove the makeup that clog my pores
take away the colored eyes
because just maybe
these dark brown eyes of mine
are just fine

remove the jewelry
do away with these clothes.
do you see me now?
no panties or bra
just me and the mirror as free as we can be
standing in my birthday suit,
my hair, my nose, my lips, my cheeks,
my arms, my breast, my stomach,
my teeth, my hips, my thighs,
my legs, even my feet,
my back and my waist line with love handles and all,
and most definitely my butt
is most perfectly formed.

so ebony, keep your korean hair
my hair may not flow down my backside or be silky
smooth,
but it's free and all mines
cover girl, you can keep your concealer
because my skin tone is just fine with me
there's no need to cover-up the natural part of me

dr. 90210 you can keep your rhinoplasty,
face lifting, lipo sucking, breast injecting
butt lifting, vagina beautifying techniques
no disrespect to you,
i must say your work is that of a true artist
but, i am already sexy as hell
thanks, but no thanks!

just uncover the true beauty of the outer me
quite frankly,
i am finally happy
with all the accessories
God gave to me.

## a nubian queen's crown

unkept
untamed
free
beautiful
it's my hair
my crown
and glory

kinky
curly
relaxed
texturized
it's my hair

my hair changes
quicker than
the four seasons
it's free to be
wild
carefree
like braids in the
shape of a crown
my crown
my hair
is free to stand tall
bold
like an afro
say it loud
i'm a nubian queen
i'm proud

it's my hair
my crown
and glory
it's not on display
for you to touch
please stop asking
my personal space
is not opened to you
this is no petting zoo
heck no
you cannot touch
my hair
for the billionth time
just stare
in admiration
of
my hair
my crown
and glory

hanging long
like a Goddess in the night
it's my hair
that's so beautifully
faded
low cut
tapper

it's my hair
my crown
and glory

well groomed

by my culture
standards
and its
perfectly
clean
purified
unfiltered
from your
prejudices
stereotypes

my crown
and glory
molded at birth
into
a nubian queen's crown

## before i awoke

i went away last night
sweetness was its name
ecstasy was its domain

dirt as white as snow

a breeze so cool and free
it ravished me
took my mind captive

played a tune for my soul to groove to

back and forth my body swung
from branch to branch
highly sprung

until the alarm awoke me

## love poem

my love for you suppresses the universe's doors
traveling into the spiritual world
there my spirit clashes
into yours
becoming soul tied
hearts smiling
what was known is now being shown
our love
growing more profound
as the seconds passes
your love
falls upon my lips
every time we kiss
i submerge myself within your heavenly touch
upon your chest i eternally
spiritually
rest
we make love without penetration,
spiritually climaxing,
mental penetration
straight to the heart
i inhale your scent
as if you are my last breath
in hopes of freezing this moment
i take a picture of your smile
with my heart trying to capture the essence of your
beauty
but it's an impossible task for
you are a divine being
with angelica wings
you loving me

me loving you
unconditionally without reason
transforming
our love into
us
he, you
me
falling hopelessly into the sweetness of you
there
i happily remain
for your love has won me under
your token of love
trust
covers my right ring finger

## love has a voice too

love speaks
we weep
before it shows, we already know
arose out of pain, confine to sorrow
until we let go of the hurt
erasing the fear
letting love in
love speaks
hearken to the voice
it knows no gender, race, or creed
only the heart
buried deep within the soul
it is the cell that begins life
dividing me into two
he and me
we are love
as love speaks
we hear, begin to listen
uncovering the clues to keep our love reproducing
love speaks
influencing my growth
removed the great wall that had me bound
physical sensation
conviction of love
love speaks
creating a bond that is spiritual
he knowing me, me knowing him
internally and externally
flaws exposed
love speaks
not hiding behind clothes

he sees me in the nude
yet, i'm not aware of my nakedness
addressing me in the eyes
we view each other soul
knowing love
understanding love
being loved
love speaks
we listen
love teach

# About the Author

"Speak it, believe it, be it." Those very words have helped transform Lacey A. Odoms' life. Ms. Odoms is a Louisianan entrepreneur and usually can be found filling orders, sourcing new products for her online lingerie boutique, Lace of Love (www.laceoflove.com), or writing poetry. She is a freelance poetry writer and speaker. *Conversations with the Heart and Soul* is her first published volume of poetry.

Ms. Odoms has been a lifelong poetry writer and first began creating works of art through her writing in primary school. While pursuing her Bachelors degree in Business Administration with a concentration in Entrepreneurship at Louisiana State University A&M, she took courses in creative writing.

With over a decade of writing poetry for speaking events and as a freelance poetry writer, Ms. Odoms has a unique powerful voice that sheds light on everyday encounters in her newest collection of poems, *Conversations with the Heart and Soul*. This collection of poems centers around love, faith, hope, social issues, and being human. Much of her writing is heavily influenced by New Orleans culture, issues experienced by individuals around the world, and her faith in Jesus Christ.

You can contact Ms. Odoms for freelance poetry writing, speaking engagements or services related to her lingerie business at <u>contact@laceoflove.com</u>.